Antonia Clare   JJ Wilson

INTERMEDIATE

Total English

Students' Book

PEARSON

Longman

Contents

Brotherly Love?

Adidas and Puma have been two of the biggest names in sports shoe manufacturing for over half a century.

Since 1928 they have supplied shoes for Olympic athletes, World Cup-winning football heroes, Muhammad Ali, hip hop stars and rock musicians famous all over the world. But the story of these two companies begins in one house in the town of Herzogenaurach, Germany.

Adolph and Rudolph Dassler were the sons of a shoemaker. They loved sport but complained that they could never find comfortable shoes to play in. Rudolph always said, 'You cannot play sports wearing shoes that you'd walk around town with.' So they started making their own. In 1920 Adolph made the first pair of athletics shoes with spikes[1], produced on the Dasslers' kitchen table.

On 1st July 1924 they formed a shoe company, Dassler Brothers Ltd. The company became successful and it provided the shoes for Germany's athletes at the 1928 and 1932 Olympic Games.

But in 1948 the brothers argued. No one knows exactly what happened but family members have suggested that the argument was about money or women. The result was that Adolph left the company. His nickname[2] was Adi, and using this and the first three letters of the family name, Dassler, he founded Adidas.

Rudolph relocated across the River Aurach and founded his own company too. At first he wanted to call it Ruda, but eventually he called it Puma, after the wild cat. The famous Puma logo of the jumping cat has survived until now.

After the big split of 1948 Adolph and Rudolph never spoke to each other again and since then their companies have been in competition. Both companies were for many years the market leaders, though Adidas has always been more successful than Puma. In the 1970s new American companies Nike and Reebok arrived to rival them.

The terrible family argument should really be forgotten, but ever since it happened, over fifty years ago, the town has been split into two. Even now, some Adidas employees and Puma employees don't talk to each other.

> **Glossary**
> [1] *spikes* = Sharp metal points that grip the ground
> [2] *nickname* = name (not your real name) given to you by friends and family

4 Mark the sentences true (T) or false (F).

1 The Dassler's father was a sportsman. ☐
2 The brothers first made sports shoes at home. ☐
3 They argued about the shoes. ☐
4 They decided to start their own companies. ☐
5 Puma sells more shoes than Adidas. ☐
6 People in the town have now forgotten the argument. ☐

5 What is the significance of the following things in the Dassler story?

> a wild cat   a river   a shoemaker   a nickname
> the 1932 Olympic Games   an argument

6 Find verbs in the text which mean the following:

1 provided a product (paragraph 1)
2 created (an institution/company, etc.) (paragraph 4)
3 moved permanently to a different place (paragraph 5)
4 be in competition with another person or company (paragraph 6)

7 Take it in turns to retell the story using the words/phrases from Ex. 5, the verbs from Ex. 6 and the pictures to help you.

Grammar | Present Perfect Simple
and Past Simple

8 a What tense are the <u>underlined</u> verbs in the sentences below?

Since 1928 they <u>have supplied</u> shoes for Olympic athletes, ...

After the big spilt of 1948 ... their companies <u>have been</u> in competition.

On 1st July, 1924 they <u>formed</u> a shoe company.

Active grammar

1 Use the <u>Past Simple</u>/<u>Present Perfect Simple</u> to describe an action that started in the past and continues in the present.

2 Use the <u>Past Simple</u>/<u>Present Perfect Simple</u> to talk about something that happened in the past but has a result in the present.

3 To include more detailed information (e.g. exact times), use the <u>Past Simple</u>/<u>Present Perfect Simple</u>.

---

b Choose the correct alternatives in the Active grammar box.

c Find two more examples of the Present Perfect Simple in the text on page 13.

see Reference page 17

9 Correct the mistakes in each sentence.

1 Has you bought those expensive shoes yet?
2 These are my favourite trainers. I've bought them last year.
3 I knew him for six years. We're still friends now.
4 Oh! You had a haircut. It's ... nice.
5 I don't have seen him for several weeks.
6 While I was in Italy I've eaten lots of pizza.

10 a Complete the dialogues using the verbs in the box. Use the Present Perfect Simple or the Past Simple.

> decide (x2) lose have (x2) find see (x2) put

A: *I've decided* to stop smoking.
B: What a great idea! When (1) _____ this?
A: Last Monday. I (2) _____ a cigarette for three days.
B: Congratulations!
A: I (3) _____ a cigar yesterday, though.
B: Oh.

C: (4) _____ my handbag? I can't find it anywhere.
D: Yes, I (5) _____ it on the table a few minutes ago.
C: Ah, here it is. I (6) _____ it! Oh no. Where are the car keys? I (7) _____ the car keys now.
D: They're on the table. I (8) _____ them there for you before breakfast.
C: Oh. Thanks.

b `1.7` Listen and check your answers.

Pronunciation

11 a `1.7` Listen again. How is *have* pronounced in a) positive sentences? b) negative sentences?

b Practise the dialogues with a partner.

Grammar | *for* and *since*

12 a Read the Active grammar box and choose the correct alternatives to complete rules 1 and 2.

Active grammar

The Present Perfect Simple is often used with *for* and *since*.

*Puma has sold shoes **for** over 50 years.*

*Adidas has sold shoes **since** 1948.*

1 We use *for* + <u>period of</u>/<u>point in</u> time

2 We use *since* + <u>period of</u>/<u>point in</u> time

---

see Reference page 17

b Do the time expressions below go with *for* or *since*?

> last night   a couple of months   this morning
> fifteen years   a while   the moment when ...
> last weekend   the day before yesterday

c Complete the sentences with *for* or *since*.

1 I've lived in the same house _____ I was born.
2 I've studied English _____ about three years.
3 I've known my best friend _____ I started school.
4 I've had the same hobby _____ over half my life.
5 I've watched four hours of TV _____ last night.
6 I've been at this school _____ a few weeks.

Person to person

13 a Make the sentences in Ex. 12c true for you and add more information after each sentence.

b Compare your sentences with other students.

Grammar | defining relative clauses

10 a Complete the extracts from the texts using the words in the box.

> who   where   which   whose   when   that

1   Ingram became one of those lucky people _____ won the big prize.
2   During the show _____ Ingram won, viewers heard someone coughing regularly.
3   He nervously looked around the studio _____ he was being filmed.
4   The man _____ fame meant that he received 500 letters a day ...
5   Whittock suffered from an allergy _____ was making him cough.
6   _____ the truth was revealed, nineteen months later, they were caught.

b Use the sentences in Ex. 10a to complete the Active grammar box.

Active grammar

*Ingram became one of those lucky people **who won the big prize**...*

... who won the big prize ... is an example of a defining relative clause; it defines exactly who or what we are talking about. This is essential information about a person, a place or a thing.

Use *who* or _____ for people
Use _____ or _____ for things or animals
Use _____ for places
Use _____ for possessions
Use _____ for time

In spoken English we often use *that* instead of *who* or *which*.
*The actress **that** stars in that film has beautiful eyes ...*

We can leave out the pronouns *who*, *which* or *that* if they are the object of the relative clause.
Quiz shows are programmes I never watch.

---

see Reference page 31

11 a Add *who*, *which* or *where* to each sentence.

1   That's the studio the last Bond film was made.
2   He's the man helps the director.
3   I've seen the film won an award at Cannes.
4   The quiz show host is the same woman reads the news.
5   Did she like the camera you bought her?
6   Here's the house I grew up.

b Which sentence in Ex. 11a doesn't need a relative pronoun?

12 Link the two sentences by using *who*, *where*, *which*, *whose*, *when* or *that*. There may be more than one possible answer.

That's the road. The accident happened there.
That's the road where the accident happened.

1   Last year I met a boy. His father is a pilot.
2   She loves the city. She was born there.
3   This is her new novel. It has already sold 500,000 copies.
4   We work for a small company. You haven't heard of the company.
5   I like the start of spring. Flowers begin to grow.
6   He's an actor. I have never seen him perform.
7   We met the artist. His exhibition was in town.
8   The children like to stay on the beach. On the beach they can play.
9   I had a great time. My cousins from New Zealand stayed with us.
10 That's the man. He won the big prize.

Speaking

13 a Play *Who wants to be a millionaire?*. Work in two groups. **Group A:** Look at page 145 and **Group B:** Look at page 148. Complete the quiz questions.

b Now work with someone from a different group. Ask your questions. If your partner answers all the questions correctly he/she wins €1 million. Count his/her score. Who is the quiz champion in the class?

Speaking

1 Discuss.

1 Do you believe everything you read in the news? Why/Why not?

2 Are some newspapers more believable than others? Which ones?

2 **a** Complete the headlines using the words below.

> saves inherits takes escapes deliver survives

1 Traffic police officer in Bangkok helps to _____ baby in car

2 Lost driver _____ a wrong turn for 5,000 miles

3 Circus monkey _____ and destroys a restaurant

4 Top chef _____ giant lobster from cooking pot

5 Sailor _____ four months at sea

6 Cat _____ £350,000 house and £100,000 from owner

b Match the headlines to the pictures. In pairs, describe what you think happened in each situation.

A

B

C

D

E

F

Reading

3 **a** Read the texts (A–F) quickly. Write the headlines from Ex. 2a above the correct story.

b Write the number of the story next to the topics below.

1 restaurants: *stories B, D* 5 food or drink

2 travel 6 babies or pets

3 animals 7 survival

4 people getting lost

c Compare your answers with a partner.

4 Read the texts again. Answer the questions.

1 a) Where did Mrs Bright want to go?
b) Why didn't she ask for directions?

2 What did Parn Hung Kuk eat for four months?

3 Why is Pooker the cat famous?

4 What damage did Lala the monkey do?

5 a) Why didn't the chef cook the lobster?
b) What did the chef do with the lobster?

6 a) What special skills does Sergeant Sakchai Kodayan have?
b) Why did the taxi driver ask for help?

A

_____

A nervous driver who went on a day-trip to Calais ended up in Gibraltar after a five-day mystery tour. Mrs Bright was planning to go to France to buy some wine. However, as she was driving around Calais looking for the supermarket, she took a wrong turn and lost her way. Without a map, and unable to speak French, she was too embarrassed to ask for directions and eventually she found herself in Gibraltar.

B

_____

A giant lobster, saved from the cooking pot by a top chef, has been returned to the sea. Chef Anton Gretzky said he was planning to serve the lobster at his expensive restaurant, but decided he couldn't boil such a fine creature. Staff from the Aquarium Restaurant in Victoria, Australia, took the lobster, named Billy, to the coast to free him. Gretzky said: 'He has been on this Earth much longer than I have.'

C

_____

Pooker, a grey and white cat, has become Britain's most famous pet. The eight-year-old cat inherited a £350,000 house and £100,000 after its owner, Mrs Rafaella Barese, died. Mrs Barese's neighbours will use the £100,000 to buy food for the lucky cat. The rich and famous always seem to make new friends easily. After just one day, two local cats were trying to move in with Pooker.

Listening

4 **a** **3.1** Listen to two families talk about their plans for a home exchange. Write 1 (Dos Santos) or 2 (Armitage) next to the activities they mention.

The Armitage family

The Dos Santos family

1	visit museums	4	go shopping
2	see cathedrals	5	visit friends
3	enjoy the local cuisine	6	sit outside and enjoy the sun

b Listen again and choose the correct alternatives.

1 **Miriam:** ... we (1) *will spend/'re spending* more than one month in London. We've never been there before.

2 **Interviewer:** I'm sure you (2) *'ll love/'re loving* it.

3 **Miriam:** And I (3) *'m going to/'m doing* do lots and lots of shopping.

4 **Interviewer:** Great. There are some wonderful shops in London. I (4) *'ll give/am giving* you the address of a great shoe shop.

5 **Jeremy:** Spain has such a rich culture ... We (5) *'ll/'re going to* see the cathedrals ...

6 **Jeremy:** Sarah and I (6) *will/are going to* enjoy the Spanish culture. And the girls (7) *will/are going to* sit outside and enjoy the sun.

7 **Jeremy:** I really hope this (8) *'ll be/is being* the holiday of a lifetime for us all.

Grammar | talking about the future

5 Match sentences 1–7 in Ex. 4b to the rules (a–d) in the Active grammar box.

Active grammar

We can use the **Present Continous**, *going to* or *will* to talk about future plans.

a) Use *going to* to talk about something **you've decided to do**. Plans can be general.
   e.g sentences: _____

b) Use *will* for a **decision made at the time of speaking**, or an **offer**.
   e.g sentence: _____

c) Use the Present Continuous to talk about **arrangements** (plans that you have already organised i.e. you have arranged the dates.)
   e.g sentence: _____

d) Use either *will* or *going to* for predictions.
   e.g sentences: _____

---

see Reference page 45

6 Complete the texts with words and phrases from the box below.

---
is going (x2) 'm starting 'll (x2)
're going won't we'll 's moving

Sarah and Jeremy

I _____ a new job in June and it's in Oxford, so I think we _____ need to move house. We'd like to buy somewhere in the countryside, so we _____ to look at some of the small villages outside the city. Unfortunately, it's very expensive around there so I'm not sure if _____ have enough money.

Miriam and Carlos

My mother _____ in with us next year, because she's old and doesn't want to stay on her own. She _____ to sell her house, which I hope _____ be too difficult. She _____ to share a room with our son for the moment. Carlos isn't too happy about this plan, but I think it _____ be great because I'll have some help with looking after the baby.

7 Correct the mistakes in the sentences. There may be more than one correct answer.

1 I'm sorry, I have to leave early. I will play squash this evening.

2 Tomorrow I go on a trip to Cambridge.

3 **A:** That's the telephone.
  B: OK. I get it.

4 Hurry up, or we're being late again!

5 **A:** Would you like a drink?
  B: Yes, I'm having a glass of water, please.

6 Will you staying here for long?

7 When I grow up, I be a firefighter.

8 We are get married in August.

9 **A:** How do I get to the airport from here?
  B: Don't worry, I'm showing you.

Person to person

8 **a** Write three or four questions to ask other students about their plans for:

> this evening   this weekend   their home
> their education/career   their (family's) future
> their next holiday

b In groups, ask and answer the questions about your future plans.

A: *Katia, what are you planning for the weekend?*

B: *I'm going to visit my aunt. She's having a party to celebrate her ...*

Listening

9 **a** Look at pictures of Jeremy and Miriam during their home exchange. What do you think the problems were? Discuss in pairs.

A

B

C

D

flat to small
no faus
loud,
music
from
neorest
bar

b **3.2** Listen and check your ideas.

c Listen again and make notes. Describe what happened.

Reading and speaking

10 Read Miriam's letter of complaint to *Yourhome-Myhome.com*. Underline the problems she talks about.

Dear Sir/Madam,

I am writing to complain about the home exchange organised by your company. I stayed in a London house, owned by Jeremy Armitage between 10 May and 6 June.

According to the information I received, the house was near the city centre. In fact, it took over two hours to get there. In addition to this, the directions for finding the house were difficult to follow and sometimes incorrect.

Unfortunately, this was not the only problem. When we arrived, the house was in a terrible mess. There were dirty dishes and cups everywhere, the bathroom was filthy, and there were no clean sheets or towels as promised. Also, the central heating wasn't working, so the house was freezing, and there was no hot water!

When I phoned your London office to explain the problems, the man who answered was very rude and unhelpful. He said that it was not possible to do anything until the house owners returned.

I am very disappointed with the standard of the house, the organisation, and the service I received in London. I expect to receive a full refund of the agency fee, and I would also like to remove my own apartment from your website.

I look forward to receiving a satisfactory reply.

Your faithfully,

Miriam Dos Santos

Miriam Dos Santos

11 Work in pairs. You are going to have a meeting between Miriam and a representative from *Yourhome-Myhome.com*.

Student A: You are Miriam. Read page 145.

Student B: You are the representative. Read page 147.

When you are ready, begin like this:

Representative: *Hello, Mrs Dos Santos. Please come in. I understand there were some problems with your home exchange.*

Writing

12 **a** Read the letter in the Writing bank on page 161 and do the exercises.

b Write a letter of complaint from Jeremy to *Yourhome-Myhome.com*. Use the pictures in Ex. 9a to help you.

Vocabulary | phrasal verbs

4   Underline phrasal verbs in the text and put them in the correct place in the diagrams.

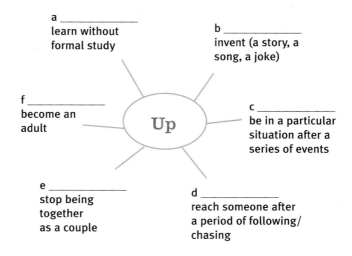

a _____
learn without
formal study

b _____
invent (a story, a
song, a joke)

f _____
become an
adult

Up

c _____
be in a particular
situation after a
series of events

e _____
stop being
together
as a couple

d _____
reach someone after
a period of following/
chasing

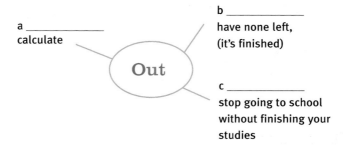

a _____
calculate

b _____
have none left,
(it's finished)

Out

c _____
stop going to school
without finishing your
studies

2   a   Answer the questions.

1   How old was Frank when he left home?

2   What did he look like?

3   How did he get his first $40,000?

4   How did he get a pilot's uniform?

5   Who was Joseph Shea? What type of person do you think he was?

6   What does Frank do now?

7   How does Frank feel about his past?

b   ◼4.1 Close your books and listen to a summary of Frank's story. Find seven more differences between the text and the summary.

1   *Frank Abagnale wasn't English. He was American.*

3   Discuss.

1   Joseph Shea said, 'I think he's a good man and a moral character.' What do *you* think of Frank?

2   Frank says, 'I thought it would be great to have a movie about my life.' Would you like a movie about *your* life? Why/Why not? Which actor would you choose to act as you?

5   One of the sentence endings is not possible. Which one?

He dropped out of (a) ~~his exams~~ (b) *school* (c) *university.*

You can drop out of school and university but not exams.

1   I broke up with (a) *my girlfriend* (b) *my relationship* (c) *my husband.*

2   They made up (a) *stories* (b) *an excuse* (c) *acting.*

3   We worked out (a) *what the problem was* (b) *the answer* (c) *wrong.*

4   She picked up (a) *Spanish very quickly* (b) *some information* (c) *a new haircut.*

5   We ran out of (a) *enough milk* (b) *money* (c) *things to do.*

6   I caught up with (a) *my studies* (b) *myself* (c) *you easily.*

7   She ended up (a) *living with me* (b) *work as a doctor* (c) *in Warsaw.*

Speaking

6   In pairs, retell Abagnale's story using the phrases below.

... his mother **broke up with** ...

... he **dropped out of** ...

... he made $40,000 . . . the banks **worked out** what he was doing

... he pretended to be ... he **picked up** the skills by reading medical books

... he **ran out of** luck in France ...

... the FBI finally **caught up with** him ...

... he **ended up** working for ...

Grammar | question tags

7 a Read the dialogues. What words go in the gaps?

1 Mr Charming: What a beautiful dress! Haven't I seen you before? You work in fashion, ___ you?
Woman: Yes, I ___. We met at a fashion show.

2 Mr Charming: I've read all your books. You've just written a new one, ___ you?
Man: Yes, I ___. It's about a film star.

3 Mr Charming: I love lobster! The food is delicious here, ___ it?
Woman: Yes, it ___. But I prefer caviar.

4 Mr Charming: You're Sarah, ___ you? No, you're Judy! Anyway, can I get you a drink?
Sarah: *I'm* Sarah!
Judy: And I'd love a drink!

5 Mr Charming: You were at the last party here, ___ you? Would you like something to eat?
Dog: Woof woof!
Mr Charming: Yes, you ___!

b 4.2 Listen and check your answers. Then practise the dialogues in pairs.

8 Read the Active grammar box and choose the correct alternatives to complete the rules (1–4).

Active grammar

When we want to confirm information, we often use question tags.

You **are** a singer, **aren't** you?*	Yes, I **am.**
You **aren't** Spanish, **are** you?*	No, I'm **not.**
You work full time, **don't** you?	Yes, I **do.**
You lived in Paris, **didn't** you?	Yes, I **did.**
They **have** arrived, **haven't** they?	Yes, they **have.**
You **can** go today, **can't** you?	Yes, I **can.**
You **would** like to see her **wouldn't** you?	Yes, I **would.**

1 To make question tags, we repeat <u>the main verb</u> / <u>the auxiliary verb.</u> *

2 If the question is in the positive, the question tag is <u>negative</u> / <u>positive.</u>

3 If the question is in the negative, the question tag is <u>negative</u> / <u>positive.</u>

4 If there is no auxiliary verb, the question tag <u>uses the main verb</u> / <u>uses *do*, *does* or *did*.</u>*

*the verb *to be* acts as an auxiliary verb in question tags

see Reference page 59

9 Add the correct tags to these questions.
1 You can speak several languages, ___? *Can't you?*
2 You work in a big company, ___? *Don't you?*
3 It's warm in here, ___? *Isn't ?*
4 You have been to the US, ___? *Yes I have.*
5 We didn't meet last year, ___? *Did we*
6 You don't like champagne, ___? *Do you*
7 You're looking for a new job, ___? *Aren't you*
8 You will be here tomorrow, ___? *Won't be you*
9 They would like a break, ___? *Wouldn't They*
10 This isn't a very good film, ___? *Is it*

10 Think about your answers to the questions in Ex. 9. Imagine you are making small talk at a party. Ask other students some of the questions.

First Conditional with *if/when/unless/as soon as*

To talk about real possibilities in the future we can use *If* + **Present Simple** + *will/can/should/may* (and other modal verbs).

*If it **rains**, I **will** stay at home.*
*If he **stays** here, he **should** learn the language.*
*If it rains I **won't** go out. If it **doesn't rain**, I **will** go out.*

Unless means *if not*.
Unless it rains, I will go out.

We use *when* to show the situation is 100% certain.
*When I **wake up** tomorrow I will make breakfast.* (it is certain that I will wake up tomorrow).

We use *as soon as* to emphasise that an event happens immediately.
*I'll tell him **as soon as** I see him.*

! We don't usually use *if* + *will* in conditional sentences.

First Conditionals can also describe events that are always true.
If trolleys are large, people will buy more. (fact)

We also often use Zero Conditionals: *If* + **Present Simple** + **Present Simple** to talk about things that are always true.
*If I **have** time, I **go** to the gym. (a fact)*
*If you **don't drink** for a month, you **die.** (scientific fact)*

Modals of obligation and prohibition

Obligation

Have to is often used for rules/regulations.
*You **have to** show your passport at Customs.* (it's a law)

Must is often used when the obligation comes from the speaker. *Must* is never followed by *to*.
*I **must** stop smoking.* (I think this)

Prohibition

Mustn't means it is prohibited/not allowed.
*You **mustn't** leave your luggage unattended.*

No obligation

Don't have to means you have a choice.
*You **don't have to** wear a suit to work.* (it's not necessary but you can if you want to)

Recommendation

*You **should** go.* (it's a good idea)
*We **shouldn't** stay late.* (it's not a good idea)

Question tags

Use question tags in spoken English to check information and to keep the conversation going.

To make question tags, repeat the auxiliary verb, not the main verb. If the main verb is *to be*, repeat that.

Affirmative statements use a negative tag.
*It**'s** cold in here, **isn't** it?*
*They **are** French, **aren't** they?*
*We **have** been there, **haven't** we?*
Use this structure when you think the answer is *yes*.

Negative statements use an affirmative tag.
*We **don't** have to pay, **do** we?*
*I **won't** be needed, **will** I?*
Use this structure when you think the answer is *no*.

If there is no auxiliary verb, use *do, does* or *did*, or their negatives.
*She **went** home, **didn't** she?*
*I **know** you, **don't** I?*

For short answers, we also use the auxiliary verb.
A: *She **doesn't** eat meat, **does** she?*
B: *No, she **doesn't**.*
A: *We **have** finished the bread, **haven't** we?*
B: *Yes, we **have**.*

Key vocabulary

Time and money
run out of   spend   lend   it's not worth the good value for   make   use your ... wisely   save   earn have got ... to spare   waste   inherit not have enough   steal   invest ... in

Phrasal verbs
drop out of   break up with   make up   work out pick up   run out of   catch up with   end up   grow up

Personal qualities
ambitious   good with figures   good with people have a sense of humour   confident   generous mean   extravagant   work long hours   tolerant know your strengths and weaknesses   flexible

Word building – opposites
succeed/fail   reward/punish   buy/sell buyer/seller   produce/consume (a product) reward/punishment   producer/consumer advertise/respond (to an advert)   success/failure advertisement/response (to an advert)

Easily confused words
rob/steal   travel/trip   fun/funny   lend/borrow remember/remind   work/job   say/tell   miss/lose

1 Complete using the correct question tag.

1 I can't park here, _____? *Can I*
2 I need to phone him, _____? *Don't*
3 The guests will be here soon, _____? *Won't be they*
4 She had a headache, _____? *Didn't she*
5 This match is boring, _____? *isn't it*
6 I'm a genius, _____? *Not I'm*
7 We're going out later, _____? *Aren't we*
8 They haven't called yet, _____? *Have They*
9 I shouldn't give her the money, _____? *should I*
10 You woke up early this morning, _____?

2 Match the questions above to these answers.

a) No, they haven't.
b) Yes, we are.
c) No, you can't.
d) No, you shouldn't.
e) Yes, it is.
f) No, you're not.
g) Yes, you do.
h) Yes, I did.
i) Yes, they will.
j) Yes, she did.

3 Some lines have one extra, incorrect word.
Write the extra word in the space. Tick (✓) if
there is no extra word.

Memo to: all staff   From: management
At the meeting we agreed on some rules.   ✓
All staff should look smart ~~to~~   *to*
at all times but workers don't never have   ___
to wear a suit unless requested. Staff   ___
must to go outside to smoke and should   ___
try not to blow smoke in through the   ___
windows. Workers mustn't not leave dirty   ___
cups in the workspaces and food must not   ___
to be consumed in the office. Staff do   ___
not have to be eat in the canteen, but   ___
lunch breaks must not have exceed 1 hour.   ___

4 Choose the correct alternative.

1 Children under 16 *don't have to / mustn't*
smoke in England. It's illegal.
2 You *don't have to / mustn't* eat if you don't
want to. It's your choice.
3 You *don't have to / mustn't* be late for work.
4 Ken's so rich he *doesn't have to / mustn't* work.
5 We *don't have to / mustn't* miss the last bus.
6 Markus *doesn't have to / mustn't* work on
Sundays but he often goes into the office.

5 Complete the sentences with *if, when* or *unless*.

1 We haven't booked our accommodation. We'll
find a hotel _____ we arrive.
2 _____ the weather's nice it's not worth going
to the park.
3 _____ you like action films, you'll love *The
Matrix*. The fight scenes are incredible.
4 I'll go home _____ you're late again tonight.
I'm tired of waiting for you.
5 She'll never pass the exam _____ she starts
working hard.
6 We'll talk about the new products _____ the
conference finishes.
7 You won't feel good _____ you do some
exercise every week.
8 I'm leaving early. I'll call you _____ I get there.

6 Correct the mistake in each sentence.

1 If I will see you tomorrow, I will give you the
book.
2 She won't act in the film unless that she
receives her normal salary.
3 We'll go as soon the taxi arrives.
4 If I drink another cup of coffee, I will be not
able to sleep tonight.
5 I can't hear you unless you don't shout.
6 When I next go shopping, I'll to buy some milk.
7 Unless you drive carefully, you won't crash.
8 As soon as you will see him, call me.

7 Complete the sentences with the words in the
box.

> advert run picked value trip up
> success figures

1 I can't even buy you a coffee because I've
_____ out of money.
2 This computer only cost me $400. Do you think
that is good _____ for money?
3 A: What's wrong with Joe?
B: He's just broken _____ with his girlfriend.
4 A: I didn't know you could speak Russian.
B: Yes, I _____ it up when I was living there.
5 My wife deals with the money for the business,
because I'm not very good with _____.
6 The show was a great _____. More than 600
people came to see it.
7 We need to find a new flatmate, so we're
putting an _____ in the local paper.
8 A: I'm flying to Paris in the morning.
B: Have a good _____!

8 a 5.5 Listen again and complete the notes.

> Hannah says:
> I didn't **expect** to see these results ... *at all*
> I **can't stand** (1) _____ *shopping*
> I **don't mind** (2) _____ *doit* the housework but it's not very interesting ...
> I'd **prefer** (3) _____ *to do* less of that kind of thing.
> I **enjoy** reading ...
> I always **look forward to** (4) _____ *start* a new book.
> I **love** cooking ...
> I **try** (5) _____ *to cook* a proper meal at least four nights a week.
> I often **invite** (6) _____ *friends* over *have* dinner ...
> I never **manage** (7) _____ *to do* much exercise.
> I never **seem** to find the time.
> That's one thing I'd **like** (8) _____ *to change*

b Look at the tapescript on page 171 to check.

Grammar | gerunds and infinitives

9 a Read the Active grammar box and put the words in **bold** from Ex. 8a in the correct column.

Active grammar

When one verb follows another, the second verb is either a **gerund** (-*ing* form) or an **infinitive** (*to* + verb).

1 Verbs always followed by the **gerund**.
 *I **can't stand shopping**.*

2 Verbs followed by the **infinitive**.
 *I didn't **expect to see** these results.*

3 Verbs followed by **object + infinitive**.
 *I **told her to call** me.*

Verb + -ing	Verb + infinitive	Verb + object + infinitive
can't stand	expect	tell

❗ Some verbs can be followed by a **gerund or infinitive**. The meaning usually changes.
 A: *I **tried to call** him but he was out.*
 B: *Have you **tried sending** him an email?*

---

b Do the same with the verbs below.

> remind   forget   agree   hate   refuse
> finish   adore   advise

see Reference page 73

10 Choose the correct alternative.

1 What hobbies would you love *to do/do* in the future?

2 Are there any activities you'd advise your classmates *doing/to do*?

3 What hobbies do you enjoy *doing/to do* in a big group? Alone?

4 Is there anything you sometimes forget *to do/do*?

5 What do you expect *doing/to do* in your free time when you are old?

6 Is there any housework that you can't stand *doing/to do*?

11 Rewrite the advertisement using the correct form of the words in brackets. Use the Present Simple.

BOOK WORLD

Would _____ (like/be) a member of a book club?
Would you like to be a member of a book club?

We (1) _____ (invite/join) BookWorld.

If (2) _____ (enjoy/read), BookWorld is for you.

You can (3) _____ (expect/receive) six free books when you join.

If (4) _____ (want/choose) your own books, we can offer great discounts, but we (5) _____ (advise/join) immediately for our special discount membership.

When you (6) _____ (finish/read) the books, you can return them!

Don't (7) _____ (forget/include) your email address. Please write in BLOCK CAPITALS.

Person to person

12 a Ask and answer the questions in Ex. 10 in groups.

b Tell other students what you found out.

5.3 | Memorable meals

Grammar	countable and uncountable nouns
Can do	recommend a restaurant

Vocabulary | food

1 Discuss.

  1 What are the worst/best meals you have ever had?

  2 Do you like food from other countries? What types of food do you like best?

2 **a** What is the difference between: *sly extra-*

  1 meal/dish?   3 dessert/side dish?   *f. e*

  2 service/tip?   4 tablecloth/napkin?   *olive*

  b Check your answers on page 146.

Reading

3 **a** You are going to read about a strange restaurant experience. Match these words from the text.

1 long	a) café
2 hungry	b) existed
3 roadside	c) road
4 delicious	d) soup
5 never	e) imagination
6 wonderful	f) and tired

  b Work in pairs. What do you think happens in the story? Use the phrases in Ex. 3a and photos to help you.

4 Now read the story to check your ideas. Why do you think the man never found the café again?

5 Find eight factual mistakes in the following summary, and correct them.

> While two engineers, who were hungry, were driving through a busy area in Iran, they stopped in a small city. They found a little café. The owner of the café, who spoke a little English, offered to serve the men a meal. The meal, which was delicious, was surprisingly expensive. After they had finished eating, the restaurant owner asked the engineers to recommend his restaurant to their friends. They did this, but the engineer's friends didn't believe it was possible to find such a poor restaurant in such a remote area. In the end, the engineer returned to the village with his wife. However, when they arrived, they couldn't find the train station. Eventually, they asked a local man about the restaurant. He said he had never heard of it, and he had been there for thirty years.

The world's best restaurant

When I was working as a civil engineer in Iran I had to visit a factory in Marinjab – the centre of a recent earthquake. Marinjab is about 150 miles from Tehran and is a quiet and isolated place. As we drove back along the long road, my colleague and I were both hungry and tired. We didn't have much hope of finding anything to eat, however, as the next town was 80 km ahead. Our only hope was of finding a small roadside café, where you are unlikely to get more than some weak tea and a little sugar to eat.

Just then we came to a village made of small huts with flat roofs. Outside one of the many huts was a sign, 'ghahvehkhaneh' (café) so we went in. It was cool inside, and there were men sitting around smoking pipes. The owner, a proud man, came in from the back and greeted us. 'Good afternoon,' he said, in perfect English. 'My name is Hosseini. My wife is Russian. We do not usually get any foreigners here. It will be a pleasure and an honour to prepare a meal for you.'

A pale-faced lady appeared with a tablecloth, and some knives and forks, shortly followed by Mr H himself, carrying a couple of bowls of soup. Made with spinach and yoghurt, and served hot, it was the most delicious soup I have ever eaten. Soon, the next course arrived – Dolmas, stuffed vine leaves. These were so delicious I asked Mr H for the recipe. He replied, 'vine leaves and rice'. It is not an Iranian dish.

The next course was a Chelo kebab – the national dish of Iran. The meat was marinated in yoghurt and spices. We ate in silence, and finished with Turkish coffee. There was something almost unreal about the atmosphere of the place. When it was time to go, we asked Mr H how much it cost, and I can tell you the price was astonishingly cheap. It was a fantastic meal – the best I have ever had, and I told him so. Mr H blushed. 'I am glad,' he said. 'As I told you, we do not see many foreigners here. Do come again, and tell your friends.'

I told a lot of friends about the meal I had, yet no one believed me. 'How could you get such a meal in such a remote place?', an English engineer friend asked me.

A few months later, I returned on exactly the same route, with this engineer friend and was determined to show him my special restaurant. We reached the village – I recognised the flat roofs – but there was no sign of the café. It was as if the building had never existed. I asked a villager. 'ghahvehkhaneh?' he said. 'There has never been one here in all the time I have been here. And that is forty years.' We drove away disappointed. Naturally, my companion laughed at me. 'You have a wonderful imagination,' he said. I don't have any explanation. I only know that I definitely had a meal in this village, in a café which, ever since, I have called 'the world's best restaurant'.

Grammar | uses of *like*

8 Match the sentences (a–e) to the correct meaning (1–5) in the Active grammar box.

a) *What would you like to do?*

b) *It tastes like chicken.*

c) *What does it look like?*

d) *What's it like?*

e) *What do you like doing on holiday?*

Active grammar

1 ***like*** (v) = to enjoy something or think that it is nice

A: _____

B: *Visiting markets and shopping.*

2 ***would like*** (v) = want

A: _____

B: *I'd like to see the statue of Molly Malone.*

3 ***look like*** (v, conj) = seem (appearance)

A: _____

B: *Like other European cities.*

4 ***be like*** (prep) = describe or give your opinion of this person/thing

A: _____

B: *It is a lively and vibrant city.*

5 ***like*** (conj) = the same way as

A: *Is that food good?*

B: _____

---

see Reference page 87

9 Complete the dialogues using expressions with *like*.

1 A: I have never been to Paris. What _____ _____ _____ ?

   B: Oh, it is a wonderful city.

2 A: What _____ _____ _____ _____ do today?

   B: I don't mind. You decide.

3 A: Have you seen the new concert hall?

   B: Yes, it _____ _____ an airport terminal!

4 A: What _____ _____ _____ most about Krakow?

   B: I love the market square with all the cafés and restaurants.

5 A: I went to that new French restaurant last night.

   B: Really? What _____ _____ _____?

   A: It was great. The food was delicious.

6 A: I am not sure if I will recognise Mr Williams. What _____ he _____ _____?

   B: He is tall, with dark hair.

7 A: Why didn't you like the food?

   B: Because it was horrible! It _____ _____ rubber.

8 A: I _____ really _____ modern art.

   B: Neither do I. The paintings often _____ _____ the work of children.

9 A: Have you seen the Sagrada Familia church in Barcelona?

   B: Yes, I thought _____ _____ _____ an enormous cake!

Person to person

10 Write three questions (using the different expressions with *like*) to ask your partner.

Who do you look like in your family?

Writing

11 a In pairs, talk about the town where you were born or a city you know well.

1 What is it like?

2 What are the people like?

3 Why do you like/dislike it?

4 What do you like doing there?

5 What would you like to change about it?

6 Does it look like any other cities that you know?

b Write a Quick Guide to a city you know well, recommending things a visitor should do. Use expressions from the text as a model.

The first place to go is ...

One of the best places to visit is ...

You mustn't miss ...

If you enjoy X, make sure you include a trip to ...

Don't leave without seeing/trying/going to ...

Finally, why not try ...?

c Share your Quick Guide with other students and read theirs. Which city/places would you like to visit? Why?

A

B

C

D

Vocabulary | describing nature

1　a Label the photos with an adjective from box A and a noun from box B.

A (desert sandy mountain
green rocky tropical)

B (rainforest range valley
coastline island beach)

b In pairs, make a list of other types of natural places.

c Discuss.

1 Could any of the places in the photos be in your country?

2 Have you ever been to any of these types of place?

3 Which is your favourite for a holiday?

Reading and speaking

2　a Describe what is happening in the pictures. What strange events/coincidences do they show?

b Read the text to find out.

3 Read the text again and answer the questions.

1 What event happened recently that inspired this text?

2 Is the text very serious, semi-serious or not serious? How do you know?

3 In your opinion, which are the most amazing events/ coincidences in the text? Which are lucky? Which could have logical explanations?

4 Have you experienced a strange event/coincidence?

4 Work with a partner. Retell the stories from the text using the key words to help.

1 family/Australian coast/whale/boat

2 dog/India/Scotland/boat

3 Karen/beach/ring

4 Roger/drowning/saved/Alice/beach/husband

Strange things happen when you travel ...

A whale jumps out of the water and on to your boat. What are the chances of that? A billion to one? There are 217 million square kilometres of ocean and the boat was only 9 metres long. But it happened last week. A family from Coventry, UK, was sailing off the Australian coast when the whale jumped on to the boat. 'Amazing!' we all say. Yes, but unbelievable events happen to travellers every day. Read about some of them below.

Some of the most incredible travellers, it seems, are pets, who may return home after years away. These stories normally involve cats, though there is a famous story of a dog that travelled 4,800 kilometres from Calcutta, India to Inverkeithing, Scotland on a boat. After several months, the boat arrived and the dog ran all the way home!

What about the things people lose and find when they are travelling? Rings are top of the list. In Hawaii, Ken Da Vico, who is a diver, says he finds about 15 wedding rings a year in the sea. He returns many of them to their owners. Even if a fish eats the ring, there is still hope. There are many cases of rings being found years later inside the stomachs of sharks, mussels and other kinds of fish. Less common is when the loser finds the lost ring, as happened when Karen Goode went to a beach in the UK and found a ring she had lost ten years before.

But the best beach story involves Roger Lausier, aged four, who was saved from drowning by a woman called Alice Blaise. Nine years later, on the same beach, a man was drowning. Roger Lausier dived into the water and saved him. It was Alice Blaise's husband.

Past Perfect Simple vs. Past Simple

Past Perfect Simple form: *had/hadn't* + past participle

Use

Use the **Past Simple** to talk about something that happened in the past, e.g. *I was ill.*

Use the **Past Perfect** to talk about what happened before that, e.g. *I had eaten something bad.*

We use it to make the order of events clear.

I was ill because I'd eaten something bad.

```
I had eaten
something bad       I was ill      now
     x                 x            x
```

I went to Bali last year. I hadn't been there before.
Her shoes were dirty. She hadn't cleaned them.

! We don't use the Past Perfect when the sequence of events in the past is clear:
I came home and turned on my computer.

The Past Perfect uses many of the same expressions as the Present Perfect (*since, for, already*):
I had worked there since 1993.
She had been my teacher for eight years.
I had already studied Spanish before I started my Italian course.

We often use *by the time* + Past Simple + Past Perfect.
By the time I arrived the party had finished.

Uses of *like*

We can use *like* to talk about:

General descriptions
What is your new school like? I have never been to that area. What's it like?

Things being similar to other things or acting in a similar way to other things
It smells like chocolate. He eats like a horse.

Physical appearance
What does he look like? Sam looks like a popstar.

Personal preferences
I like fresh coffee. Harry doesn't like swimming.

A specific preference for the future
I would like a non-smoking seat, please.

Looks like also means 'seems'.
It looks like Rachel is going to be late again!

Articles

a/an

1 When it's the first time we've mentioned the subject.
   Last night I saw a ghost!
2 With jobs. *She's a doctor, he's a cook.*

the

1 When we already know which one we are talking about (it has been mentioned previously).
   What did the ghost look like?
2 The subject is unique (there's only one).
   The President of the USA.
3 With superlatives. *It's the best film.*

No article

When we make generalisations with:

a) plural nouns. *Trousers are warmer than skirts.*
b) uncountable nouns. *Progress is possible.*

Articles in place names

We use **no article** with:

1 Most place names. *Warsaw, Spain*
2 Names with South/East, etc. *South America*

We use **the** for:

1 Countries with the word State, Kingdom or Republic.
   the United States, the United Kingdom
2 Plural names. *the West Indies*
3 Rivers, seas, oceans, deserts. *the River Seine*
4 Describing where in a country. *the south of France, the west coast of Scotland*

Key vocabulary

Travel
adventure/package/beach/camping/sailing holiday
sightseeing tour   safari   (river) cruise   go abroad
new experiences and sensations   local culture
go sightseeing   famous landmarks   barren deserts
cultural and historical capitals   have fun and relax
independent travel   unforgettable journey

Places to visit in a city
castle/palace   museum/art gallery   pub/café
park/garden   lake/fountain   bookshop/library
shop/market

Places to visit (nature)
sandy beach   tropical rainforest   rocky coastline
desert island   mountain range   green valley

Expressions with *get*
get hungry/dark/worse/cold/wet/ill/bored
get a newspaper/a drink   get a letter/an email/
a distinction/a job/directions   get home/to the
airport   get someone from the station/a taxi
get on/get back/get on (with)
get married/dressed/lost

1 Choose the correct alternative.

When I got to the restaurant I realised that I *left*/ ~~*had left*~~ her phone number at home.

1 By the time she was eighteen she *lived/had lived* in six cities.

2 On my birthday, when I *got/had got* home I found that my husband *had cooked/cooked* dinner.

3 That morning, she got up, had breakfast and *went/had gone* to work, as normal.

4 Tibet was incredible. I *never saw/had never seen* such a beautiful country before.

5 He called twice but no one answered. They *all went/had all gone* to bed.

6 When I arrived in France, my cousins *kissed/ had kissed* me on the cheek.

7 When I returned a month later, I found that the weather *grew/had grown* cold and I *had/had had* to buy a new jacket.

8 It was Max! I *hadn't seen/didn't see* him for twenty-five years.

2 Put the words in order.

to you Would something eat like ?

Would you like something to eat?

1 is What like it ? been there haven't I before .

2 like I at prefer but films I watching going cinema to the home .

3 looks sister you like think Don't her Maria ?

4 to what see wait finished the house will look when like I it is can't .

5 early Tim up getting doesn't like .

6 Would have drink in like you come a to and ?

7 like your is job new What ?

8 my Do like hairstyle you new ?

9 a I walking in new I around am like when city .

10 tickets 'd like exhibition, two please for the I .

3 Do these use *the* or not?

the Black Sea

1 Canary Islands

2 Africa

3 Czech Republic

4 Andes mountains

5 River Nile

6 Canada

7 United Arab Emirates

8 northern Europe

9 Atlantic Ocean

10 Mount Kilimanjaro

11 Sahara Desert

12 Mediterranean Sea

4 Choose the correct alternative.

A: Why do you like this hotel so much?

B: It's *a hotel*/~~*the hotel*~~ where I met Dave.

1 A: How was the restaurant?
   B: *The food/Food* was wonderful.

2 A: Why don't you go to Australia for your holiday?
   B: I don't like *the aeroplanes/aeroplanes*.

3 A: Who was Alexander Fleming?
   B: He's *a/the* man who discovered penicillin.

4 A: Why didn't you buy a dog?
   B: *The cats/Cats* are easier to look after.

5 A: What happened yesterday?
   B: (a) *The/A* strange man knocked on our door and asked for water.

6 A: Why does Mariana always win prizes?
   B: Because she is *the most/most* intelligent person in the class.

5 Complete the advertisement by choosing the correct word (a, b, c or d).

Would you like to (1) __go__ abroad? Would you like to (2) _____ the world? If you are only interested in (3) _____ a tan and lying on a (4) _____ beach with all the other tourists, then AMAZ Tours are not for you. We organise trips to the (5) _____ rainforest in Brazil. Here you will have a chance to learn (6) _____ new cultures and to experience something truly different. The Amazon is (7) _____ smaller and smaller. See it before it disappears. If you want to stay longer than a month we will even help you (8) _____ a job. We fly every Saturday. It takes fifteen hours to get (9) _____ and a whole lifetime to leave! (10) _____ your ticket before 12th July and we will give you a 15% discount!

1 (a) get (b) see (c) *go* (d) have

2 (a) visit (b) see (c) travelling (d) find

3 (a) get (b) have (c) being (d) getting

4 (a) sand (b) sandy (c) deep (d) heavy

5 (a) tropic (b) deep (c) whole (d) tropical

6 (a) about (b) in (c) over (d) at

7 (a) become (b) getting (c) now (d) grown

8 (a) getting (b) to (c) get (d) for

9 (a) over (b) us (c) arrive (d) there

10 (a) Have (b) Make (c) Get (d) Do

11 Read the text and circle the correct form.

Going to school

I didn't (1) *used to/use to/did* like the journey to school. I (2) *wouldn't/would to/would* go by bus, but I was afraid of the other children. They were bigger than me, and they (3) *used to/wouldn't to/would to* shout at me. I always sat at the back of the bus, even though it (4) *would be/used to be/used be* the hottest place, and I (5) *wouldn't/didn't use to/would* hope that no-one could see me. It's funny to think that those boys were probably only eight years old, but I (6) *would be/used to be/used be* so frightened.

12 a Complete the sentences using *use(d) to* and a suitable verb from the box.

> live not watch be like not behave do not go eat

1 Did your life _____ very different when you were a child? How?
2 I _____ playing outside with my friends.
3 I _____ TV in the evenings.
4 We _____ in the countryside, but now I live in Vienna.
5 My family _____ to the seaside at the weekend.
6 Did you _____ ice cream every day?
7 My best friend at school was called Sam. We always _____ our homework together.
8 I _____ very well at school.

b Change the sentences so that they are true for you and answer the questions.

c Compare your answers with a partner.

Pronunciation

13 **7.3** Listen to the sentences. How are *used to* and *didn't use to* pronounced? Which letters are silent? Repeat the sentences.

Speaking

14 a Think about a good (or bad) teacher from your past. Use the questions to help you write a few notes.

1 What did he/she look like? What clothes did he/she use to wear?
2 What subject did he/she use to teach?
3 What did he/she use to do that was so special/bad?
4 Did all the students particularly like/dislike this teacher? Why?
5 How did this teacher treat you personally? Was he/she very different from the other teachers you had?
6 Would you like to meet him/her again? What would you say to him/her now?

b Tell other students about your teacher.

Writing

15 Look at the Writing bank on page 163 and complete the exercises.

16 Write an entry for the website below about a favourite teacher from your past.

GREAT TEACHERS

| Log-in | News | Events |

The College of Education is compiling stories of great teachers and the qualities that made them memorable. You can help by submitting a memory of your special teacher below.

• Your favourite teacher's name:

• What is the first characteristic that you think of when you remember this teacher?

• Describe a specific memory of this teacher:

• Describe how this teacher treated you as a student:

Grammar	modals of ability, past and present
Can do	talk about abilities in the past and present

Vocabulary | old age

1 Match the words in **bold** in sentences (1–4) to the definitions (a–f) below.

1 At what age do people **retire** in your country?
2 Do **senior citizens** get a **pension**?
3 Is it common for **elderly** people to live in **nursing homes** in your country?
4 Do young people generally **respect** the old in your country?

a) a place where old people go to live and be looked after (n)
b) old people (n)
c) old (used to describe people) (adj)
d) money you receive (from the government or your employer) after you stop working (n)
e) stop working because of your age (v)
f) treat them like important people (listen to them and appreciate them, etc.) (v)

Listening

2 **7.4** Listen to three people discussing three of the questions in Ex. 1. Which questions do they talk about?

Part 1: _____

Part 2: _____

Part 3: _____

3 **7.4** Listen to the conversations again and circle the correct phrase.

1 In Ghana, old people *are involved in family decisions /often ask their children for help.*
2 In England, old people *can do some things for free /have to pay the same as young people.*
3 When people get old in Ghana, they *live in nursing homes /live with extended family.*
4 Nursing homes in England *can be very good/ are usually very bad.*
5 In Africa, old people usually *retire at 65 /don't retire.*

4 In groups, discuss the questions in Ex. 1.

Reading

5 a Read the texts about some remarkable people. Work in pairs. **Student A:** read the texts below. **Student B:** turn to page 150. As you read, make notes about the following:

> Name age activity/achievement
> personal philosophy/attitude to being old

b Tell your partner about the three people.

It's never too late ...

Ella Scotchmer, 104

Ella took up solo travelling at the age of 96, touring the USA for three months on a Greyhound bus. She enjoys dancing, and has recently taken up tai chi.

'I don't think I look my age, so people don't believe I'm 104. Up until a couple of years ago, I was still bowling and swimming and doing all manner of things. I can't remember how many cruises I've been on since I turned 100. I've done the Norwegian fjords, the Canaries, the Caribbean. In the future, I'd still like to go to Mexico, and I haven't been to Malta or Gibraltar yet. I'll just have to wait and see what happens.'

'I don't think I look my age, so people don't believe I'm 104.'

Elizabeth Collins, 94

Elizabeth Collins is the wife of the famous British artist Cecil Collins, but she is also an artist herself. In her nineties, she was able to sell some work to the Tate Gallery, London.

'When my husband died eight years ago it made work easier – although in some ways much harder. Alone, you can easily get into a negative hole. But I think my painting now is wiser, more understanding about life, and innocent. It's not about being old; you paint when you have time or possibility. I have that possibility now. I've thought of dying quite a lot. I like the idea. But it's got to be the right time. I walk into the traffic all the time without looking. I could get hit but I don't. Obviously, it's not the right time for me yet.'

4 Discuss.

1 What is the writer's attitude to the new laws in New York, and to the mayor? Is the article 100% serious? How do you know?

2 Do you think the laws in the article are 'stupid'?

3 Would these laws be popular in your country?

4 Should smoking be banned in all public places?

5 Which is more important – individual freedom, or health and safety for everyone?

Grammar | Second Conditional

5 Read the Active grammar box and choose the correct alternatives.

Active grammar

*If more cities **had** these laws, America **would** be a better place to live.*

*If people **smoked** in here, **we'd** go home smelling of cigarettes.*

1 Use the Second Conditional to describe an imaginary situation / a real situation in the present or future and its result.

2 In the *if* clause, use the Present Simple / the Past Simple.

3 In the result clause, *would* (or *'d*) is used because the situation is in the past / imaginary (hypothetical).

4 It is possible to use a modal verb such as *could* or *might* instead of *would*, if you are certain / not sure of the result.

First and Second Conditional:

In a real situation use the First Conditional / Second Conditional.

In a hypothetical situation use the First Conditional / Second Conditional.

The First Conditional / Second Conditional uses the Present Simple + *will*.

The First Conditional / Second Conditional uses the Past Simple + *would*.

---

see Reference page 115

6 Make Second Conditional sentences using the verbs in brackets.

1 If you _____ (be) a New York police officer, _____ (arrest) someone for feeding birds?

2 I _____ (not like) the new laws if I _____ (live) in New York.

3 Where _____ (go) if you _____ (want) a cigarette at work?

4 If the laws _____ (not make) money, they _____ (not exist).

5 I _____ (not be) very happy if I _____ (have to) pay a fine for using two subway seats.

6 If New York _____ (not have) these laws, tourists _____ (find) it dangerous and dirty.

7 If these laws _____ (exist) in your country, _____ (be) popular?

8 There _____ (be) less crime if the police _____ (have) more power in my country.

7 Talk to a partner. Are the situations in the box real/possible situations in your life or imaginary? In what circumstances *would/will* you:

---

lie to a police officer   miss my English lesson
live in another country   go away next weekend
stay in bed until 12.00p.m.   take a taxi
make a long distance phone call
write to the government   sing in public
run a marathon/five km

I would lie to a police officer if I was a criminal!

I will miss my English lesson if I have too much to do at work.

Pronunciation

8 a 🔲 8.1 Underline the word you hear.

1 A: Where *would/will* you go with all that money?
   B: To Hawaii.

2 A: She's got four brothers, hasn't she?
   B: I *didn't/wouldn't* know that. I don't know her very well.

3 A: So who wants to do the shopping?
   B: *I'll/I'd* do it, but I have to do my homework.

4 A: Is it possible to get some help? The job *wouldn't/won't* take very long with three of us.
   B: You're asking for help? That makes a change!

b Practise the dialogues with a partner.

Speaking and listening

9 a Work in groups. If you could propose five new laws for your town, what would they be?

b Tell the class about your laws/proposals and together, choose the five best.

'If we could propose one new law, we'd stop cars from entering the city centre.'

10 a **8.2** Listen to four speakers talking about things they would like to change about their city. Match the speaker to a subject: a) noise, b) buildings, c) pollution or d) disabled facilities.

1 Gabriel (Mexico City) _____
2 Luciana (São Paulo) _____
3 Clive (Manchester) _____
4 Olivia (Naples) _____

b Listen again. Complete the extracts below.

> 1 Mexico City has too many cars, _____ it's really polluted. So, if I could change one thing, I'd have a law against all the traffic. I'd stop cars from going into the city centre.

> 2 I'd improve the facilities for disabled people. People in wheelchairs have real problems _____ _____ the roads and pavements. Even in public buildings sometimes there are no elevators _____ they can't use the rooms on the higher floors.

> 3 There's no peace and quiet here. All the noise and mess is _____ _____ these students. They scream and shout every night. _____ I would make some new laws against all the noise so we could get some sleep!

> 4 _____ _____ the stupid laws here, everybody builds these terrible buildings. They are really ugly, _____ _____ the city isn't so beautiful these days. If I was mayor, I would pass a law to stop these buildings.

c Check with the tapescript on page 174 .

11 a Read the How to ... box. Put the formal expressions below in the correct place.

1 *Therefore, ...*
2 *This leads to* (+ noun or gerund) *...*
3 *As a result of* (+ noun) *...*
4 *As a result, ...*

HOW TO ...

talk about cause and result

Describe cause	*It's caused by* (+ noun or gerund) ... *because* (*of*) _____
Describe result	*so ...* *which means ...* _____ _____ _____

b In written English which words or expressions can start a sentence? Which words/expressions can join two clauses?

c Complete the sentences.

1 Tourists love Venice, so ...
2 London is very expensive, which means ...
3 Many travellers like Brazil because of ...
4 Parts of Africa are very hot. Therefore, ...
5 As a result of ..., Saudi Arabia is a rich country.
6 Many tourists don't understand the culture of the countries they visit. This leads to ...
7 English is the language of tourism. As a result, ...
8 The pollution in many cities is caused by ...

Writing

12 a Read the article in the Writing bank on page 164 and do the exercises.

b Choose one of the laws you proposed in Ex. 9. Write an article for a newspaper about the issue you'd like to change.

b Listen again. Who says these phrases? Write the letter R (Roger), T (Tunde) or S (Sarah).

1 'I stopped work a year ago ...'

2 'My family wanted me to work in the family business ...'

3 'All I thought about was making money for my family.'

4 'We ... sold our house, left our jobs, and said good-bye to our friends.'

5 'I had always dreamed of going to study in another country ...'

6 '... it changed our world completely.'

7 '... we just fell in love with the house the moment we saw it.'

8 '... maybe I'll change career and start my own business.'

9 'I met my fiancée, Nancy, here, and we are planning to get married ...'

c Check your answers in the tapescript on page 174.

d Which speaker do you think had the most difficult decision to make? Why? Tell a partner.

Grammar | Third Conditional

4 a Read the sentences and answer the questions.

If I had stayed at work, I wouldn't have spent time with Jack when he really needed me.

1 Did Roger stay at work?

2 Did he spend time with Jack?

I wouldn't have met Nancy if I hadn't come to France!

3 Did Tunde come to France?

4 Did he meet Nancy?

b Look at the Active grammar box and choose the correct alternative to complete the rule.

Active grammar

Use the Third Conditional to talk about a <u>real</u>/<u>hypothetical</u> situation in the <u>present</u>/<u>past</u>.

Form the Third Conditional with:

If + subject + past perfect + *would(n't) have/could(n't) have* + past participle.

If I had stayed at work, I wouldn't have spent time with Jack.
Past condition   Past result (hypothetical)

or

I would've cooked dinner, if I'd known you were coming.
Past result (hypothetical)   Past condition

In spoken English, *have* and *had* are usually contracted to *'ve* and *'d* (see example above).

see Reference page 115

5 a Match the sentence beginnings (1–8) with the endings (a–h).

1 If I had known the test was today,

2 I wouldn't have missed the last train

3 If I'd known it was you on the phone,

4 If you'd asked me out to dinner,

5 I wouldn't have felt so tired this morning

6 If I hadn't gone on holiday to Greece,

7 I would have organised a party for you

8 I wouldn't have spent so much time with my children

a) if I'd gone to bed earlier.

b) I'd have said 'yes'.

c) I would have done some revision.

d) if I'd known you were coming.

e) I would've answered it.

f) if I hadn't stopped work.

g) if I had left home earlier.

h) I wouldn't have met my husband.

b **8.5** Listen and check.

6 Write Third Conditional sentences using the prompts.

I didn't know Mary was ill.
I didn't send her any flowers.

If I had known Mary was ill, I would have sent her flowers.

1 Taxis were very expensive. We didn't take one.
2 They didn't ask anyone for directions. They got lost.
3 The weather wasn't very good. We didn't enjoy the holiday very much.
4 It was raining. They crashed the car.
5 I didn't see you when you passed me in the street. I didn't say 'hello'.
6 I wasn't hungry. I didn't eat lunch.
7 I didn't know that Eva had to get up early. I didn't wake her.
8 I didn't like my History teacher. I gave up History.

Pronunciation

7 **a** 8.6 Listen to this sentence. Which words are contracted?

If I had left home earlier, I wouldn' t have missed the train.

b Listen to the rhythm of the sentence. Do the stressed words fall with a regular beat in the sentence?

8 **a** 8.7 <u>Underline</u> the stressed words in these sentences.

1 If I'd known the test was today, I would've done some revision.
2 If I'd gone to bed earlier, I wouldn't've felt so tired.
3 If you'd asked me out to dinner, I'd've said 'yes'.

b Listen and check. Practise saying the sentences using the same rhythm.

Speaking

9 **a** Draw two large circles in your notebook and label one of them 'Now' and the other 'Ten years ago'. Read the questions and write short answers in the 'Now' circle.

1 Where are you living?
2 Who is your closest friend?
3 What do you do?
4 How do you spend your time?
5 Do you spend much time with your family?
6 Are you studying?
7 Do you play any sports?
8 What music do you enjoy?
9 What are your dreams/ambitions?

b Change the questions in Ex. 9a to make questions in the past. Write short answers for these questions anywhere in the 'Ten years ago' circle.

10 Show your circles to a partner. Tell them about how much your life has changed in the past ten years. Ask questions to find out as much information as possible.

11 Discuss.

1 What have been the important turning points (important moments or events which have changed things) in your life?
2 How might your life have changed if these turning points had been different?
3 Do you think you have always made the right decisions?

Writing

12 Write a paragraph describing an important turning point in your life and the effect this had. Think about what happened before/after the event, and how things might have been different.

Word building

1 Add some examples of prefixes to the table below.

PREFIX	MEANING	EXAMPLE	YOUR EXAMPLES
over-	too much	**over**cook	
under-	not enough/below	**under**developed	
dis-	not/separate	**dis**honest	
in-/im-	not	**in**human	

2 Complete the text using prefixes.

Life CHANGE

Many people _dislike_ their job. Maybe they are (1) _____ worked or (2)_____ paid. Maybe they feel (3)_____ valued in the company or they (4)_____ agree with the company's methods. If you are one of these people, why not change things? LifeCHANGE workshops show you how to be (5)_____ dependent. You will see (6)_____ credible differences in your life as your problems (7)_____ appear. Change is never (8)_____ possible, but you have to make the first move.

Call us on **0879 997 5543** for an (9)_____ formal chat.

3 Add some examples of suffixes to the table below.

SUFFIX	EXAMPLE	RULES	YOUR EXAMPLES
-tion/-ation	crea**tion**, civili**sation**	If the verb ends in -e, cut the -e. If the verb ends in -se, the suffix is usually -isation.	
-ence/-ance	intellig**ence**, ignor**ance**	There are no clear rules about which words end in -ence or -ance. You have to learn them!	
-ment	move**ment**	Add -ment to the verb.	
-ness	dark**ness**	If the word ends in -y, change the -y to -i. happy → happ**i**ness	

4 Complete the text by adding suffixes to the words in bold.

Vote for the Perfect Party.

1   Our priority is **educate**.
2   We will increase **employ**.
3   We promise to give free **accommodate** to people over 65.
4   There will be free hospital **treat** for everyone.
5   We promise proper **punish** for criminals.
6   We believe in the **important** of free speech.
7   Giving you, the voter, your **independent**.
8   A **govern** for the 21st century.
9   Taking the country in a new **direct**.
10 Your vote can make a **different**.

5 **a** Choose one of the topics below and make some notes on it.

an inspiration

new forms of entertainment

globalisation

a great achievement /my greatest achievement

what happiness means to me

cultural difference

my development

b Work with two or three other students. Speak for about a minute on your topic using your notes to help you.

c Change groups. EITHER speak about the same topic more fluently, OR choose a new topic. What new things did you learn about your classmates?

Listening

12 a **9.3** Listen to the interview and choose the correct option.

1 He says that a) he has a lot of problems b) he likes talking about his problems c) people like talking to him about their problems.

2 He tells her that he a) works hard b) hardly works c) doesn't like work.

3 He says that a) he is organised b) he is disorganised c) he likes organising things.

4 He tells her that a) he doesn't panic b) he often panics c) he doesn't have a calm character.

5 He says that a) he finds working on his own difficult b) he likes working with people c) he doesn't like to work from home.

b Put the words in the correct order to make questions from the interview.

1 good people are listening at you to ?

2 usually solutions find difficult you can to problems ?

3 weaknesses do what and you think your strengths are ?

4 work you do pressure well under ?

5 working own on do like you your ?

c Match the questions (1–5) above to the reported questions (a–e) below. Complete the sentences.

a) She asked him whether he liked working on his _____.

b) She asked him what his _____ and _____ were.

c) She asked if he could usually find _____ to _____.

d) She asked him whether he was good at _____.

e) She asked him if he worked well under _____.

d Listen again. What did Mr Wilkins reply to each question?

13 Read and complete the Active grammar box.

Active grammar

We use the verb *ask* to report questions.

We use *if* or *whether* to report <u>Yes/No questions</u> / <u>Wh- questions</u>.

Direct question	Reported question
'_____ you like working in an office?'	I **asked** her if/ **whether** she liked working in an office.
'_____ is your name?'	I **asked** her what her name was.

see Reference page 129

14 Write questions 1–6 in reported speech. Start with 'She asked me ...'.

1 Are you good at organising people?

2 Do you enjoy working in a team?

3 What do you do when your ideas don't work?

4 Do you listen to other people's advice/ suggestions?

5 What do you do when you have too much work?

6 What time do you normally start work?

15 There are mistakes in some of the sentences below. Find the mistakes and correct them.

1 Anna said me that she would be back by five o'clock.

2 Mara told me to switch the computer off.

3 My brother asked to wait for him at the station.

4 The driver told he was feeling sick.

5 The shopkeeper asked if we needed help.

6 Her husband said her that she could use his credit card.

Person to person

16 a Write five questions to ask your partner to find out if he/she would make a good manager.

Do you like ...? Are you good at ...? What ...? Can you ...? Do you ...?

b Interview your partner. Would he/she make a good manager? Why/Why not? Report what your partner said back to the class.

I asked Maria if she prefers working on her own or in a team, and she told me she likes ...

Reading and speaking

1 Discuss.

1 What do you think are the best and worst things about being famous?

2 Would you like to be famous? What for?

2 Read the text and answer the questions.

1 What was Jane and Denise's dream?

2 How did they achieve it?

3 What problems did they have?

Operatunity

(a) _____

Operatunity is a TV talent show for amateur opera singers. The winners get the chance to sing with the English National Opera. When two housewives, Denise Leigh and Jane Gilchrist won in 2002, their lives changed forever. As they sang Verdi's *Rigoletto* at the Coliseum in Rome, they were transformed from working mothers into opera celebrities.

(b) _____

'I live in the village I was born in,' says Denise, who is blind. 'Lots of my neighbours are family, and my life revolved around my three children.' Jane, who worked as a cleaner and a shop assistant, was in a similar situation. She says, 'All I had to look forward to was seeing my four children grow up, and I love that, but ... you think "there must be more to life". Winning *Operatunity* has opened up avenues I never knew existed.'

(c) _____

'This last year has been amazing,' Denise continues. 'Last month was Paris, before that we were recording at Abbey Road, in London, and recently we had our album launch at the Royal Opera House.' 'We've been treated like princesses,' laughs Jane. '... champagne, chocolates, five-star hotels ...'

(d) _____

But it wasn't all so easy. For Denise, the worst part was waiting at the beginning. 'After I'd sent in my application form I worried for a month. Then I had to wait ten days after my first audition. That was awful.' Even when they won the competition they were allowed to tell their close family but they weren't allowed to tell anyone else until later. Denise and Jane also found the travelling difficult. They couldn't take their children with them while they were away singing so they had to organise childcare. However, there's been no problem with the physical side of singing: 'We didn't have to worry about that as we've had lots of help and wonderful voice training,' says Jane. They also had to learn to deal with the media. 'The kids loved the fact that they could stay up and watch us on TV, but I just couldn't understand why some newspapers were more interested in the fact I divorced at 21, rather than the fact I had just sung at the Coliseum,' says Denise.

(e) _____

When asked if they'd recommend the experience, Denise says, 'It's been the most fantastic thing I've ever done. I wake up in the morning and think I must be the luckiest person in the world. My profession is something I used to do as a hobby.' And their advice to other hopeful singers out there? 'Live your dream,' says Jane. Denise agrees: 'If you think you can do it, then try it. No one else is going to do it for you.'

3 a Match the headings below to the paragraphs (a–e). <u>Underline</u> the phrases in the text that helped you.

> The difficult parts
>
> Living the new life
>
> The competition
>
> Their lives before
>
> Advice

b Summarise each paragraph in just one sentence.

4 Correct the eight mistakes in the summary.

Jane and Denise won a pop singing competition on the radio, even though Denise is blind. The competition gave them the opportunity to sing a famous Beatles' song at Wembley Stadium, and it changed their lives forever. Although they are both housewives with families – Denise has three children, and Jane has two – they now get the chance to travel and see the world, singing. Their new lives have not been very exciting, and they have been treated very well. They found the travelling easy because their children were at home. They would recommend the experience to other singers, and say that if your dream is to sing, you should keep it as a hobby.

5 Discuss.

Would you ever enter/consider entering a competition like *Operatunity*? Why/Why not?

Grammar	review of past tenses
Can do	say different types of numbers

A

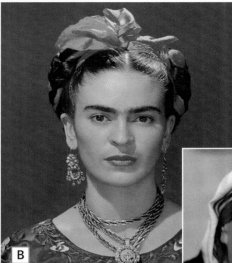

B

C

D

E

Listening and speaking

1 Who are the women in the photos? Do you know anything about them? In what areas did they 'shape' the 20th century?

2 **a** [10.3] Listen and check. Why are the women famous?

b Listen again and complete the notes.

1 Mother Teresa helped the sick in India. Her charities are found in more than _____ countries.
2 Marie Curie worked with _____, and won the Nobel Prize in 1903 and _____.
3 Frida Kahlo was famous for her amazing and unusual _____.
4 Marilyn Monroe starred in _____ films.
5 Rosa Parks refused to give up her bus seat. She went to _____ because of this.

Vocabulary

3 **a** According to the listening texts, which of the women:

1 **encouraged** black people to fight for their rights? _____
2 was a very **brave** woman? _____
3 was a **talented** actress? _____
4 **dedicated her life** to helping the sick? _____
5 was **determined** to survive and made a remarkable recovery? _____
6 was a **brilliant** scientist? _____
7 was **involved in** a serious accident? _____
8 **inspired** many other people to start caring for others? _____

b Match the words in **bold** to the words/phrases in the box.

> had courage   was a great example to   never stopped trying
> excellent   played a part in   spent all her time
> very good at something   made people want to do something

4 Complete the sentences with a suitable word/phrase from Ex. 3a.

Frida Kahlo encouraged people to believe in themselves.

1 Rosa Parks' actions have _____ people all over the world to fight for equality between the races.
2 Mother Teresa was _____ _____ charity work in India and saved thousands of lives.
3 Marilyn Monroe was _____ to become a film star.
4 Marie Curie _____ _____ _____ to science.

5 Can you think of any other 'heroes' of the 20th century? Choose two people. What qualities did they have? Tell other students who you chose and why.

Reading

6　**a**　Read about another famous woman of the 20th century. Stop at each question and, with a partner, guess the answer. Then follow the instruction.

　b　When you know who the famous person is, write her nickname in the gap in the title.

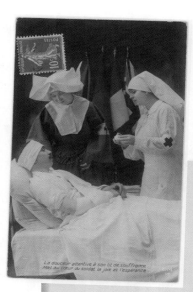

La douceur attentive à son lit de souffrance
Met au cœur du soldat la joie et l'espérance

1 She was born in a home for poor people in Saumur, France, on 19 August 1883, and christened Gabrielle. Her mother died when she was just six years old. This left her father with Gabrielle and four other young children. What happened next?

　a) The father brought them up alone.

　b) The children became film stars.

　c) The father sent them away.

Read 5 to find out ⋯⋯⟩

7 She had worked for a short time as a nurse in World War I, but during World War II she went to Switzerland. She returned to France in 1953 and dressed many Hollywood stars such as Liz Taylor and Katharine Hepburn. What happened next?

　a) She acted in a film about her life.

　b) She died in the 1970s.

　c) She moved to the West Indies.

Read 4 to find out ⋯⋯⟩

The Making of _____

4 She was still working up until her death on January 10, 1971, when her fashion empire brought in over $160 million a year. Before that, in 1969, Katharine Hepburn had starred in a Broadway musical about her life. She is considered one of the most influential fashion designers of the 20th century.

THE END

5 He sent them away to grow up with relatives. In her early twenties, while she was working as a singer in cafés, she met two wealthy men, one a soldier, the other an Englishman called Arthur Capel. What did the men do?

　a) They shot each other because they loved her.

　b) They helped her start a clothes business.

　c) They paid for her to travel around the world.

Read 3 to find out ⋯⋯⟩

3 With the men's money and contacts, she opened a hat shop in 1913. She soon expanded her business to include clothes, and opened a fashion shop at 31 rue Cambon, Paris. What happened next?

　a) She married a politician.

　b) She became a singer.

　c) She designed clothes for women.

Read 6 to find out ⋯⋯⟩

6 She began to design clothes for women. She said, 'Most women dress for men and want to be admired. But they must also be able to move, to get into a car. Clothes must have a natural shape.' What was her other famous product?

　a) Shoes.

　b) Perfume.

　c) Furniture.

Read 2 to find out ⋯⋯⟩

2 In the early 1920s she introduced Chanel No. 5, which became one of the world's favourite perfumes. Throughout the 1920s and 30s her clothes were becoming more and more popular. But then, in 1939, World War II began. What happened to her?

　a) She moved to Switzerland.

　b) She designed uniforms for soldiers.

　c) She worked as a nurse.

Read 7 to find out ⋯⋯⟩

Listening

7　**[10.4]** Listen to a summary of the woman's life. The speaker gets three facts wrong. Which facts?

8　In pairs, retell the woman's life story using these numbers/dates.

> August 19, 1883　six years old　two men
> 1913　31 rue Cambon　No.5　1920s and 1930s
> 1939　1953　1969　January 10, 1971　20th
> century　$160 million

Communication activities

Lesson 2.1 | Ex. 1, page 20

The order in which they were invented is: newspapers, radio, TV, video, the Internet.

Lesson 2.2 | Ex. 13a, page 25

Group A

Complete the quiz questions with the correct relative pronoun.

Category: Sport

1 The football player _____ won the World Cup when he was seventeen years old was
(a) Pelé (b) Maradona (c) David Beckham (d) Ronaldo
(€100,000)

2 The boxer _____ went to prison for refusing to fight in the war against Vietnam was (a) Joe Frazier (b) Muhammad Ali
(c) George Foreman (d) Sugar Ray
(€100,000)

3 The USSR is the only country _____ team has beaten the US in the Olympic Games at (a) baseball (b) basketball (c) volleyball
(d) swimming (€100,000)
[answers: 1a, 2b, 3b]

Category: The Arts

1 A haiku is a type of poem _____ has
(a) 14 lines (b) a male hero (c) 3 lines (d) a description of an animal (€100,000)

2 Jackson Pollock was one of the artists _____ invented
(a) Cubism (b) Action Painting (c) Surrealism (d) Impressionism
(€100,000)

3 The place _____ Mozart, Haydn and Johann Strauss were born is
(a) Germany (b) Switzerland (c) Poland (d) Austria
(€150,000)
[answers: 1c, 2b, 3d]

Category: Geography

1 The name of the desert _____ extends across Mongolia and Northern China is
(a) The Sahara Desert (b) The Gobi Desert (c) The Kalahari Desert
(d) The Arabian Desert
(€100,000)

2 The name of the river _____ flows both north and south of the Equator is (a) The Congo (b) The Nile (c) The Mississippi
(d) The Amazon
(€100,000)

3 The canal _____ joins the Red Sea and the Mediterranean Sea is
(a) The Rhine Canal (b) The Panama Canal (c) The Suez Canal
(d) The Egyptian Canal (€150,000)
[answers: 1b, 2a, 3c]

Communication 2 | Ex. 1, page 30

Students A

You want to make money for your newspaper. You like celebrities on the front page. You don't like too many disasters or too much international news, because you don't think it sells well.

Now look at the list of stories in Ex. 2a on page 30.

Lesson 3.1 | Ex. 11, page 36

Student A

You want:
- a full refund of the €500 fee.
- more money because you had to buy sheets and towels.
- a written apology from *Yourhome-Myhome.com*.
- to take your home off the website.

Lesson 5.1 | Ex. 13a, page 64

Problems

1 Your hotel has been receiving complaints from the customers: the lifts are too slow. They are very old, expensive lifts with material on the walls. The cost of buying new lifts is extremely high, and the hotel doesn't have enough money. Think of a solution.

2 You work in a university hospital. You want to persuade the students to get an injection against tetanus. You have been sending brochures to the students for one year, but only 3% of the students have come for an injection. Another university hospital has been doing the same thing, but 28% of their students have had injections. They've been sending out one extra piece of paper with the brochure. What is on this piece of paper?

Communication activities

Lesson 4.3 | Ex. 3, page 54

Student B

How you are persuaded to spend more by ...

Supermarkets ...

We spend more time in them than we want to, we buy 75 per cent of our food from them and we buy a lot of products that we don't even need.

Supermarkets always have good marketing ideas. When shopping baskets were introduced in the 1950s stores, they were an immediate success. Now shoppers could walk around and pick up items they previously didn't even look at. Soon came trolleys, and the bigger the trolley, the more people will buy. Customers think 'If I buy lots now, I won't need to come back later.' Supermarkets help us enjoy shopping by making the environment pleasant. They play music to help us relax and blow air from the in-store bakery around the shop. Some stores have 'greeters' to welcome you. This gives the illusion of community – the notion that shopping in a giant store isn't so different from visiting a village shop.

Warning signs:

- Two for one deals: Supermarkets will usually offer these when a fruit or vegetable is in season, and so there is a lot of it, and it's cheap.
- Music: If the experience is relaxing, you will stay in the shop longer. The longer you stay, the more you buy.
- The influence of smell: As soon as you walk into the shop, you can smell the bread and coffee smells. Pleasant aromas can make you buy more.

Communication 2 | Ex. 1, page 30

Students B

You are responsible editors. You want a lot of news about developing countries. You think that major disasters and international news stories are very important. Now look at the list of stories in Ex. 2a on page 30.

Lesson 5.3 | Ex. 2b, page 68

Meal – a time when you eat food. For example, lunch.
Dish – food that is prepared in a special way. E.g. Roast beef.
Service – the help people give you in a hotel/restaurant. It may be included in the price.
Tip – extra money you leave if you think the service is good.
Dessert – a dish you eat it at the end of the meal, often sweet.
Side dish – a dish you eat with your main course, e.g vegetables.
Tablecloth – the large cloth which covers the table.
Napkin – a smaller cloth which you use to clean your mouth.

Lesson 7.1 | Ex. 10b, page 92

Quiz answers

Quiz A

1 Who painted Guernica in 1937? Picasso
2 When did Mozart start composing music? When he was 4 years old/1760
3 Who discovered penicillin in 1928? Sir Alexander Fleming
4 Which of the world's greatest scientists lived from 1879–1955? Albert Einstein
5 Which famous city is nicknamed The Big Apple? New York
6 What invention is Guglielmo Marconi responsible for? The radio
7 Which is the largest desert in the world? The Sahara
8 Who earned $34 million per day during the 1990s? Bill Gates
9 Which country is the oldest surviving republic in the world? San Marino
10 When did Boris Becker become the youngest man ever to win the men's singles at Wimbledon? 1985

Vocabulary 5 | Ex. 5, page 71

Student A

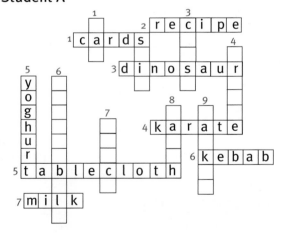

Lesson 6.3 | Ex. 11, page 84

Student A

Read these sentences to your partner and continue the conversation. (Invent a response!)

My cousin knows Harrison Ford!

My best friend has been married five times!

My partner is famous!

I eat pasta every single day!

I left home when I was fifteen!

I won the lottery last year!

1 Describe the properties in the photos and answer the questions.
1 Would you like to live in any of these places? Why/Why not?
2 What do you think are the advantages or disadvantages of living in each place?

2 Watch the film extracts. What do the speakers say about where they live? Make notes in the table below.

	Description of property/area	Good/bad things about where they live	Where they plan to live in the future
Speaker 1			
Speaker 2			
Speaker 3			
Speaker 4			

3 Discuss.
1 Do you agree with what the speakers say about living in the city/country?
2 Would you prefer to live in the city or the country? Why?

4 Tell your partner about where you live and what you like/dislike about it.

My Fair Lady

The Great Gatsby

Trading Places

The Count of Monte Christo

1 Discuss.

1 Have you seen any of the films in the photos?

2 What is the connection between them?

3 How did the people in the films become rich?

4 Do you know any other films with a 'rags to riches' theme?

2 **a** You are going to watch a film extract from *The Lavender Hill Mob*. Read the quotes from the extract below and check the meaning of any words you do not understand. Use a dictionary if necessary.

1 'It's your first visit to South America?' __

2 'Yes, I wish I could stay longer.' __

3 'Congratulations! A wonderful party! The President himself told my husband it was the occasion of the year.' __

4 'Thank you, señor. Always so generous.' __

5 'You rode a very good race.' __

6 'You run along and get yourself a little birthday present.' __

7 'You seem to have accomplished quite a lot in one year.' __

8 'For twenty years I've dreamed of a life like this.' __

9 'Most men who long to be rich know inwardly that they will never achieve their ambition.' __

10 'It was my job to supervise the deliveries of bullion from the gold refinery to the bank.' __

b Watch the film and match the quotes to the people below.

A

B

C

4 Put the events from the film extract into the correct order.

a He gives a jockey (someone who rides horses) some money. __

b He remembers when he was working hard in the city. __

c He donates money to 'Victims of the Revolution'. __

d He gives someone money for a birthday present. __

e He gives the waiter a tip. __

5 Discuss.

1 What type of film is *The Lavender Hill Mob?*

2 Who is the main character?

3 Where is he in the extract?

4 How do you know he is very wealthy?

5 How do you think he became rich?

6 Who is he telling his story to?

7 What do you think is going to happen to him now?

Irregular verbs

Verb	Past Simple	Past Participle
be	was/were	been
beat	beat	beaten
become	became	become
begin	began	begun
bend	bent	bent
bet	bet	bet
bite	bit	bitten
blow	blew	blown
break	broke	broken
bring	brought	brought
build	built	built
burn	burned/burnt	burned/burnt
burst	burst	burst
buy	bought	bought
can	could	been able
catch	caught	caught
choose	chose	chosen
come	came	come
cost	cost	cost
cut	cut	cut
deal	dealt	dealt
dig	dug	dug
do	did	done
draw	drew	drawn
dream	dreamed/dreamt	dreamed/dreamt
drink	drank	drunk
drive	drove	driven
eat	ate	eaten
fall	fell	fallen
feed	fed	fed
feel	felt	felt
fight	fought	fought
find	found	found
fly	flew	flown
forget	forgot	forgotten
forgive	forgave	forgiven
freeze	froze	frozen
get	got	got
give	gave	given
go	went	gone/been
grow	grew	grown
hang	hung	hanged/hung
have	had	had
hear	heard	heard
hide	hid	hidden
hit	hit	hit
hold	held	held
hurt	hurt	hurt
keep	kept	kept
kneel	knelt	knelt
know	knew	known
lay	laid	laid
lead	led	led
learn	learned/learnt	learned/learnt
leave	left	left
lend	lent	lent

Verb	Past Simple	Past Participle
let	let	let
lie	lay	lain
light	lit	lit
lose	lost	lost
make	made	made
mean	meant	meant
meet	met	met
must	had to	had to
pay	paid	paid
put	put	put
read/riːd/	read/red/	read/red/
ride	rode	ridden
ring	rang	rung
rise	rose	risen
run	ran	run
say	said	said
see	saw	seen
sell	sold	sold
send	sent	sent
set	set	set
shake	shook	shaken
shine	shone	shone
shoot	shot	shot
show	showed	shown
shrink	shrank	shrunk
shut	shut	shut
sing	sang	sung
sink	sank	sunk
sit	sat	sat
sleep	slept	slept
slide	slid	slid
smell	smelled/smelt	smelled/smelt
speak	spoke	spoken
spell	spelled/spelt	spelled/spelt
spend	spent	spent
spill	spilled/spilt	spilled/spilt
split	split	split
spoil	spoiled/spoilt	spoiled/spoilt
spread	spread	spread
stand	stood	stood
steal	stole	stolen
stick	stuck	stuck
swear	swore	sworn
swell	swelled	swollen/swelled
swim	swam	swum
take	took	taken
teach	taught	taught
tear	tore	torn
tell	told	told
think	thought	thought
throw	threw	thrown
understand	understood	understood
wake	woke	woken
wear	wore	worn
win	won	won
write	wrote	written

Pronunciation bank

Part 1 | English phonemes

Consonants

Symbol	Key word	Symbol	Key word
p	**p**an	s	**s**ell
b	**b**an	z	**z**ero
t	**t**ie	ʃ	fre**sh**
d	**d**ie	ʒ	mea**s**ure
k	**c**ap	h	**h**ot
g	**g**ap	m	**m**et
tʃ	**ch**urch	n	**n**et
dʒ	**j**udge	ŋ	ra**ng**
f	**f**ew	l	**l**ed
v	**v**iew	r	**r**ed
θ	**th**row	j	**y**et
ð	**th**ough	w	**w**et

Vowels

Symbol	Key word	Symbol	Key word
iː	f**ee**t	aɪ	**by**
ɪ	f**i**t	aʊ	br**ow**n
e	b**e**t	ɔɪ	b**oy**
æ	b**a**t	ɪə	h**ear**
ɑː	b**a**th	eə	h**air**
ɒ	b**o**ttle	ʊə	s**ure**
ɔː	b**ou**ght	eɪə	pl**ayer**
ʊ	b**oo**k	əʊə	l**ower**
uː	b**oo**t	aɪə	t**ired**
ʌ	b**u**t	aʊə	fl**ower**
ɜː	b**ir**d	ɔɪə	empl**oyer**
ə	broth**er**	i	happ**y**
eɪ	b**ay**	u	ann**u**al
əʊ	g**o**ld		

Part 2 | Sound-spelling correspondences

In English, we can spell the same sound in different ways, for example, the sound /iː/ can be 'ee', as in *green*, 'ea' as in *read* or 'ey' as in *key*. Students of English sometimes find English spelling difficult, but there are rules and knowing the rules can help you. The chart below gives you the more common spellings of the English sounds you have studied in this book.

Sound	Spelling	Examples
/ɪ/	i	this listen
	y	gym typical
	ui	build guitar
	e	pretty
/iː/	ee	green sleep
	ie	niece believe
	ea	read teacher
	e	these complete
	ey	key money
	ei	receipt receive
	i	police
/æ/	a	can pasta land
/ɑː/	a	can't dance*
	ar	scarf bargain
	al	half
	au	aunt laugh
	ea	heart
/ʌ/	u	fun sunny husband
	o	some mother month
	ou	cousin double young
/ɒ/	o	hot pocket top
	a	watch what want
/ɔː/	or	short sport store
	ou	your course bought
	au	daughter taught pause
	al	bald small always
	aw	draw jigsaw lawyer
	ar	warden warm
	oo	floor indoor
/aɪ/	i	like time island
	y	dry shy cycle
	ie	fries die tie
	igh	light high right
	ei	height
	ey	eyes
	uy	buy
/eɪ/	a	lake hate shave
	ai	wait train straight
	ay	play say stay
	ey	they grey obey
	ei	eight weight
	ea	break
/əʊ/	o	home phone open
	ow	show throw own
	oa	coat road coast
	ol	cold told

* In American English the sound in words like *can't* and *dance* is the /æ/ sound, like *can* and *man*.

Part 3 | Weak forms

In English, some words have two pronunciations – the strong form and the weak form. We usually use the weak form when the word is not stressed. Most of these words are 'grammar' words e.g. *a, an,* *than, have, been,* etc. Knowing weak forms helps you understand spoken English. The chart below shows some common weak forms.

Word	Strong form	Weak form	Examples of weak forms in sentences
the	/ðiː/	/ðə/	He's **the** person who cleans our office.
was	/wɒz/	/wəz/	He **was** an architect.
were	/wɜː/	/wə/	They **were** born in France.
been	/biːn/	/bɪn/	I've **been** to San Francisco.
do	/duː/	/də/	Where **do** you live?
does	/dʌz/	/dəz/	Where **does** he work?
have	/hæv/	/əv/	What **have** you got?
has	/hæz/	/əz/	Where **has** she been?
had	/hæd/	/həd/, /əd/	He **had** already gone. He'd already gone.
can	/kæn/	/kən/	She **can** sing very well.
to	/tuː/	/tə/ (before consonants)	I prefer **to** go home for lunch.
at	/æt/	/ət/	Let's meet **at** six o'clock.
of	/ɒv/	/əv/	There's a lot **of** food.
for	/fɔː/	/fə/	He's away **for** two months.
from	/frɒm/	/frəm/	She's **from** Brazil.
than	/ðæn/	/ðən/	She's taller **than** Juan.
could	/kʊd/	/kəd/	Where **could** I go?
would	/wʊd/	/wəd/əd	What **would** you do?
should	/ʃʊd/	/ʃəd/ʃd	What **should** I have done?

Part 4 | Silent consonants

Some letters appear in words where they are not pronounced.

Letter	Silent in:	Letter	Silent in:	Letter	Silent in:
b	dou**b**t clim**b**	h	**h**our w**h**at	p	**p**sychology recei**p**t
c	**sc**issors **sc**ene	k	**k**now **k**nee	s	i**s**land ai**s**le
d	We**d**nesday san**d**wich	l	ta**l**k ca**l**m	t	lis**t**en whis**t**le
g	ou**g**h**t** lon**g**	n	autum**n** colum**n**	w	**w**rite ans**w**er

really looking forward to it.

Dialogue 3

Woman: I joined the gym about three months ago and it's made a real difference to my life. It was difficult at first ... you know there were times when I just wanted to go home and watch TV ... but it quickly became part of my daily routine. I feel so much better now. I've got so much more energy ... and I've made a lots of new friends too.

Dialogue 4

Girl: I think it depends really. Some people need a routine. Babies, older people ... perhaps. They like to do everything in the same way, in the same order. I don't know. I think life is probably a bit boring if you always do that, but it depends. My granddad had a very strict routine. He always ate at the same time and went to bed at the same time, and it worked for him, but it's not for everybody, is it?

Dialogue 5

Man: Well, I don't want to stay in my present job for too long, that's for sure. And I certainly don't want to settle down at the moment either. I'm always looking for new experiences ... new places to go ... new people to meet ... so yes, I think it's true to say that I like change!

Unit 9 Recording 1

Speaker: Good afternoon everybody. Today I'd like to tell you about our idea for a new business. We want to open a restaurant that serves food from all over the world. Our main idea is that the chefs cook food from fifty or sixty countries. The most important thing for us is that the food is great. We'll allow the chefs to choose the dishes and the menu will be very big, with something for everybody. We'll employ three chefs and six waiters. We won't make the waiters wear a uniform, and they will have one special perk: we'll let them eat free at our restaurant. To sum up, our restaurant will be small and friendly but with a great international menu. The name of the restaurant is World Food! Thank you for listening. Are there are any questions?

Unit 9 Recording 2

Speaker 1

I find her really annoying. She comes in at the end of the day, and gives you lots more work to finish by tomorrow. It makes it very difficult to organise your time.

Speaker 2

I am very pleased to work for Anya. She is a great boss, and very understanding. Like when my wife was ill in hospital, she sent her flowers. And when I was feeling worried about it, she sent me home for the day. I didn't have to ask, because she understands how you feel before you say anything.

Speaker 3

He can be quite aggressive. If someone forgets to do something, he really shouts. Sometimes he even throws things around the office. It can be very frightening.

Speaker 4

It's very exciting to work with Michael because he has so much energy and enthusiasm. He has a lot of new ideas for the business, and he involves people, so that their ideas are included too. Work never gets boring because he is always changing things.

Unit 9 Recording 3

I=Interviewer   W=Mr Wilkins

I: So Mr Wilkins you've applied for a management position. Let me ask you a few questions.

W: Yes, fine.

I: Firstly, are you good at listening to people?

W: Yes, I think so. People often talk to me about their problems and ask me for advice, and things. So yes.

I: Their problems? That's interesting. And can you usually find solutions to difficult problems?

W: Well, actually, not always. No. I usually ask other people for their ideas. If there's a problem at work, for example, I ask my colleagues for ideas, and then try a few different ideas to see which one works.

I: That's good. So you listen to other people's ideas?

W: That's right.

I: And what do you think are your strengths and weaknesses?

W: Well, I'd say that my strengths are that I work very hard. I'm very motivated. And I'm good with people, so I get on well with my colleagues. My weakness is probably that I'm a bit disorganised. My desk is always a mess, and I tend to arrive late for meetings.

I: I see. And do you work well under pressure?

W: Yes. Quite well. I'm a calm person by character, so if there's a problem I don't panic. As I said before, I like to work hard, so if there's a lot of work to do, I'm happy to just keep working until it's finished. I'll get up very early in the morning, or just work all night until the job's done. That's not a problem.

I: OK. And do you like working on your own?

W: Umm ... that's a difficult one. I like working with people, as I said. That's the part of the job I enjoy best. But if there is a difficult document or report to write, then I work well on my own. Sometimes I'll work from home, so that there are no interruptions, so then I work on my own.

I: That's great. Well, thank you for taking the time to come and see us Mr Wilkins ...

Unit 9 Recording 5

1 In an international company it is useful to be able to speak more than one language.

2 Our company is very hi-tech so you need to be able to use a range of computer software.

3 A good salesperson can give good presentations.

4 I have to work accurately because mistakes are very expensive

5 People get very stressed when they continually work under pressure.

6 Many people work irregular hours in my company – some start early and some finish late.

Unit 9 Recording 6

Speaker 1

Air hostess: You have to be good at dealing with people. Some people get nervous about flying, or they feel ill. Or sometimes there are arguments between passengers, so you need to listen to people and solve these types of problems. Also, sometimes you have to persuade people to do things they don't want to do, like sit in a different seat... . Um ... I suppose ... it's useful to speak more than one language. And of course you have to like travelling! I travel thousands of kilometres every week.

Speaker 2

Office manager: I found that you needed to prioritise. There were so many things to do – you had to say, 'This is important. I'll do this first'. And then you had to delegate, find other people to do some of the jobs. We worked under a lot of pressure, and we worked irregular hours too. Sometimes we couldn't go home until midnight. That was fairly common. Other things: well, it was useful to be able to type fast. And we used a whole range of computer software. So, yeah it was kind of one of those jobs ...

Speaker 3

Medical scientist: You had to work accurately. And also you had to be very good with figures. You couldn't make mistakes. It was different when I was doing the job, but these days they use a lot of computer software. In fact most of the work is done by computer. And this helps with solving problems, because often you don't get the result you are looking for, and you don't know why.

Speaker 4

Bus driver: You need to be able to drive well obviously, and also to be patient. That's the most important thing. What else? Well, we sometimes get stuck in traffic jams. Y'know, it's a hot day and you're in the middle of the city, and you're stuck there for an hour. Well, they get angry. Other drivers. Passengers. So we have to deal with these people. And then sometimes we work irregular hours – at nights or early in the morning. That's a bit of a pain in the neck but y'know someone's gotta do it ...

Unit 9 Recording 7

1 She first learned soccer from her teacher at high school.

2 We went to a restaurant near the shopping centre. As usual, I paid the bill.

3 For my holiday I bought a return ticket to Paris.

4 There's a place on the freeway where we can stop and buy gas.

5 If you want to use the toilet, we can go to my flat. I live close to here.

6 I never get any mail, only stupid text messages on my cell phone.

7 Let's get some burgers and fries and go watch a movie.

8 A: How are you getting to the mall?

Tapescripts

B: On the subway.

9 Excuse me. I'd like the check, and could you show me where the restroom is, please?

10 There's a restaurant by the underground station which sells great fish and chips.

Unit 10 Recording 1

J=Jack A=Alice

J: Have you got a good memory?

A: I wish I had! I'm a disaster! I'm good at remembering things like appointments and meetings at work. That's fine. But I'm terrible with faces and names. It happens all the time that I meet people and I immediately forget their name.

J: Me too. I'm hopeless. I can never remember faces. The other day I was walking along the street and this man came up and said hello. And I had no idea who he was.

A: And who was he?

J: He was my boss's husband.

A: Oops.

J: Very embarrassing. What about dates? Do you remember people's birthdays, that kind of thing?

A: Well, I'm OK with birthdays because I write them all down in my diary. I wish I didn't have to, but ... y'know.

J: And phone numbers?

A: I can't even remember my own phone number half the time.

J: Personally, I wish I could remember things like writers' names or the names of songs. It happened quite recently that we were talking about books and I'd read an excellent novel and I wish I'd remembered the name because I wanted to recommend the book. But I just couldn't remember it.

A: What book's that then?

J: Um, I can't remember the title.

Unit 10 Recording 3

N=Narrator

N: Mother Teresa dedicated her life to helping street children and sick people in India. She started the Missionaries of Charity to help people in need. Her hard work and dedication inspired many other people to start caring for others. Now over one million people work for her charities in more than 40 countries.

N: Marie Curie was a brilliant scientist. Originally from Poland, she went to study in France and worked at the Sorbonne University with her husband, Pierre. Together, they discovered radiation. She won the Nobel Prize in 1903 and 1911.

N: Frida Kahlo was a gifted painter from Mexico. She was famous for her amazing and unusual paintings. At age 18, she was involved in a serious accident in which she nearly died. But she was determined to survive and made a remarkable recovery. Many people admired her for her colourful and lively personality.

N: Marilyn Monroe was a talented actress who was loved by people all over the world. She overcame many problems in her life to become one of the twentieth century's greatest cultural icons. Although she died quite young, she had already starred in thirty films during her career and is particularly remembered for her charm and beauty.

N: Rosa Parks, a black American, was a very brave woman. In Alabama in 1955, she refused to give her bus seat to a white woman. She was then arrested and sent to prison. People were so angry about this that they stopped using the buses for nearly a year. She encouraged many other black people in America to fight for their rights. Many of America's laws were changed because of her protest.

Unit 10 Recording 4

Narrator: Coco Chanel was born in France in 1883. Her father died when she was a child and her mother sent the children away to grow up with relatives. When she was a young woman Chanel met two rich men who helped her to start her business. She opened her first shop in 1913, where she sold perfume. Soon afterwards she opened a shop in Paris and began designing clothes. Her clothes and perfume business did very well until 1939, when she left France to go and live in Hollywood. In 1953 she returned to France. She dressed many famous film stars and she was still working when she died in 1971. She is considered one of the most influential designers of the twentieth century.

Unit 10 Recording 6

Dialogue 1

Man: So, thank you very much for coming, everybody. I hope you found the talks interesting and useful. If you want any more information, you can find us on our website. The address is in the programme, so do send us an email. Thank you and goodbye.

Dialogue 2

F=Father D=Daughter

F: OK, you've got everything? Passport, ticket, money.

D: Yeah, I think so. Let me just ...

F: Have you got the address where you're staying?

D: Yes.

F: Your mobile?

D: Yeah, it's right here.

F: So you'll give us a call when you arrive.

D: Yeah, it'll probably be late this evening.

F: OK, have a safe trip.

D: Thanks, Dad.

F: And we'll see you in a couple of weeks.

D: Two weeks. OK, bye.

F: Bye, darling.

Dialogue 3

M=Man W=Woman

M: Are you off now?

W: Yep.

M: Have a good weekend.

W: You too. Bye.

M: Bye.

Dialogue 4

M=Man W=Woman

M: Thanks for everything. I really enjoyed it.

W: You're welcome. Come back any time.

M: Thanks a lot.

W: Maybe see you next weekend. There's a party at Joe's.

M: Oh OK, yeah, sounds good. Alright then, thanks. Bye.

W: Take care.

Unit 10 Recording 7

Leaving on a jet plane

All my bags are packed
I'm ready to go
I'm standing here outside your door
I hate to wake you up to say goodbye
But the dawn is breaking
It's early morn
The taxi's waiting
He's blowing his horn
Already I'm so lonesome
I could cry

CHORUS
So kiss me and smile for me
Tell me that you'll wait for me
Hold me like you'll never let me go
I'm leaving on a jet plane
Don't know when I'll be back again
Oh babe, I hate to go

There's so many times I've let you down
So many times I've played around
I'll tell you now, they don't mean a thing
Every place I go, I'll think of you
Every song I sing, I'll sing for you
When I come back, I'll wear your wedding ring

(CHORUS)

Now the time has come to leave you
One more time
Let me kiss you
Then close your eyes
I'll be on my way
Dream about the days to come
When I won't have to leave you alone
About the time I won't have to say

(CHORUS)

Unit 10 Recording 8

1 Ouch!
2 Yuk!
3 Shh!
4 Mmm!
5 Phoo!